The Coral Reefs of Florida

VOLUME 2
OF THE FLORIDA WATER STORY

Peggy Sias Lantz and Wendy A. Hale
Illustrated by Jean Barnes

Pineapple Press, Inc.
Sarasota, Florida

To my mother, who first taught me to love the written word. —Peggy Lantz

To Nikki and Chris, and our family's love of the sea. —Wendy Hale

To Mikey and in memory of Ruth E. and Albert G. Wilson —Jean Barnes

TABLE OF CONTENTS

Copyright © 2014 by Peggy Sias Lantz and Wendy Hale
Illustrations © 2014 by Jean Barnes

Inquiries should be addressed to:
Pineapple Press, Inc.
P.O. Box 3889
Sarasota, Florida 34230

www.pineapplepress.com

First Edition
10 9 8 7 6 5 4 3 2 1

Design by Carol Tornatore
Illustrations colorized by Jennifer Borresen
Printed in the United States

Library of Congress Cataloging-in-Publication Data
Lantz, Peggy Sias, author.
    The coral reefs of Florida / Peggy Sias Lantz and Wendy Hale. — First edition.
        pages cm. — (The Florida water story series ; volume 2)
    Summary: "Under the blue-green water near the Florida Keys lies a magical world that few people see. The only coral reefs in North America are home to billions of tiny coral animals, schools of colorful fish, graceful sea turtles, and other fascinating creatures. Come explore the rainbow-colored coral reefs of Florida and discover who lives in the living garden that is coral."—Provided by publisher.
        Audience: Ages 10–14.
        Audience: Grades 7 to 8.
        ISBN 978-1-56164-703-3 (pbk. : alk. paper)
    1. Coral reef biology—Florida—Juvenile literature. 2. Coral reef ecology—Florida—Juvenile literature. 3. Natural history—Florida—Juvenile literature. 4. Coral reefs and islands—Florida—Juvenile literature. I. Hale, Wendy, 1954– author. II. Title.

QH95.8.L36 2014
578.77'8909759—dc23
                                                  2014010160

Coral Reefs

Under the blue-green water near the Florida Keys lies a magical world that few people see. It is a beautiful garden—a world of gorgeous colors, feathery plumes waving in the currents, creatures swimming, floating, crawling, or gliding everywhere you look.

These gardens are Florida's coral reefs, and they are places alive with activity—home to billions of tiny coral animals, schools of colorful fishes, graceful sea turtles, and other fascinating creatures.

But coral reefs are more than beautiful places admired by the snorkelers and scuba divers who swim here. Their solid, rocklike shapes form a barrier that protects Florida's coast from storm waves and provides boats with a safe place to anchor nearby. Fish and lobsters live in the reef's nooks and crannies, providing food for us and a livelihood for the people who catch them.

A mask and snorkel or a ride on a glass-bottomed boat are ways you can look down into this beautiful garden. This book will introduce you to some of the amazing creatures that live on the coral reefs of Florida.

What Is Coral?

Though some coral may look like boulders or feathery leaves, coral is neither a rock nor a plant, but a colony of living animals.

An individual coral animal is called a polyp. Each polyp is tiny—from the size of a pinhead to a thumbnail across, depending on the species.

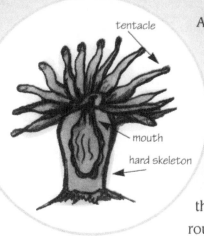

tentacle

mouth

hard skeleton

Although they are small, polyps are easily visible to snorkelers or swimmers with goggles. Coral polyps live inside a limestone cup they make themselves.

One end of a polyp's tube-like body is firmly attached to a hard surface. The opposite end is the animal's mouth, which is surrounded by a ring of tentacles that wave about in the ocean currents.

What's a Reef?

It's hard to believe that something as large as a coral reef could be built by tiny coral polyps no bigger than your fingernail! But each individual polyp helps the reef to grow by secreting a hard limestone cup around itself. When it grows large enough, it connects with the cups of nearby polyps, forming a continuous mat of living tissue—a reef. As the coral polyps crowd together, the reef grows larger and larger.

When coral polyps die, their soft body parts decay, but the hardened cups are left behind. New polyps then build their cups on top of the dead cups.

Coral reefs grow very slowly. It has taken thousands of years to build the reefs found in Florida.

---

colony   a group of the same kind of animal living together.
polyp   a marine animal with a tubelike body which is attached at one end to a hard surface and which has a mouth at the other end.

secrete   to release a substance.
species   a kind of plant or animal.
tentacles   a ring of food-gathering appendages surrounding the mouth of some marine animals.

Kinds of Reefs

Different kinds of coral grow in all the oceans of the world, but polyps need special environmental conditions to grow into huge reefs like those in Florida. Animals other than coral polyps can form reefs, too, and so can things that don't live naturally in the ocean (like shipwrecks and old tires).

Coral reefs

Coral polyps can grow into different reef shapes. In Florida, the most common are patch and bank reefs. Patch reefs are small "patches" of coral, usually surrounded by sea grasses. Near the Florida Keys, bank reefs grow parallel to the coast. Here, large growths of coral are separated by "valleys" of sand and coral rubble. Water currents pass through these valleys, bringing food to the coral polyps, and fish and other animals use the valleys as underwater "highways."

Worm reefs

A different kind of reef, called a worm reef, grows off the east coast of central Florida. These reefs are made by tropical marine worms instead of coral polyps.

Like the coral reefs, worm reefs also grow in shallow water not far from the coast. They are made up of tubes of sand grains cemented together by a gluelike material produced by the worm. The reefs grow larger as the larvae of the worms settle onto the existing masses of tubes.

Artificial reefs

Artificial reefs are made up of materials that are put in the sea by people, either by accident or on purpose. Shipwrecks and wrecked airplanes, bridge pilings and fishing piers, pipelines and navigation markers are all examples of artificial reefs.

Many of these large structures dumped in the sea haven't moved for many years, and communities of reef creatures have grown on and around the pieces of metal, wood, or concrete. Artificial reefs create places for algae, sponges, and corals to attach to, while animals that move, such as spiny lobsters, stone crabs, and fish, live nearby.

algae   certain plants that usually live in water.
larva   the immature form of an animal that is very different from its adult form.

rubble   pieces of broken coral.

Where Does Coral Grow?

To grow into reefs, corals need clear, salty, warm water—almost as warm as your bath water. Because they don't like cold water, coral animals can live only in shallow, sunlit areas of tropical and subtropical oceans. The only place along the entire North American continent that meets these conditions is the Atlantic coast south of Miami. Here, the Florida reefs extend about 290 kilometers (180 miles) along the Florida Keys past Key West to the Dry Tortugas.

Reefs do not grow along Florida's Gulf coast because the water is cooler and less clear, but individual corals, sometimes called coral heads, can grow as far north as Cedar Key.

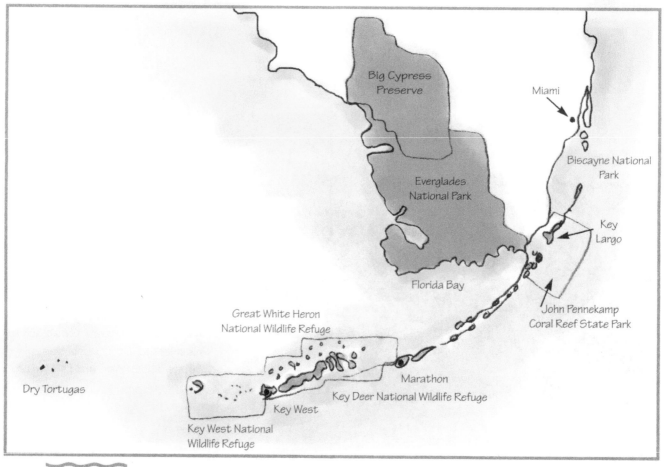

subtropical situated in the region of the earth lying between the tropics and temperate lands (cooler than the tropics, warmer than the temperate areas).

tropical situated in the tropics, a part of the earth's surface near the equator, where it is very warm.

How Does Coral Eat?

A polyp waves its tentacles outside its cuplike home, sweeping the water to catch food floating in the ocean currents. When food brushes the tentacles, special stinging cells called nematocysts stun the prey and capture it. Then the tentacles pull the food into the polyp's mouth. Coral animals feed upon plankton, floating organic materials, and even tiny fish.

How Does Coral Protect Itself?

Polyps feed at night, when—with masses of tentacles waving in the water—coral can look like a huge mound of fuzz! But during the daytime each polyp pulls its body almost completely inside its cup home, just like a turtle. This helps to keep it safe from grazing fish and other coral predators.

Another way a polyp protects itself is by oozing a slimy mucus that covers it and its neighbors. This mucus coating cleanses the polyps of silt and sand that could smother them.

graze to feed on vegetation.
mucus a slimy protective secretion.
nematocysts stinging cells in tentacles of coral polyps, jellyfish, and anemones.
organic made of living (or formerly living) plants or animals.

plankton microscopic plants and animals that drift in the sea.
predator an animal that hunts, kills, and eats other animals.
prey an animal that is eaten by another animal.

Kinds of Coral

The many different species of coral that grow in Florida waters can be grouped into two kinds, depending on the type of cup they secrete—hard corals and soft corals.

Hard corals

The rocklike structures that eventually build up into a reef are the hard corals. Hard corals grow in many different sizes and shapes, and are often named for things they look like.

Staghorn coral

Staghorn coral is one of the major reef-building corals in Florida. It grows like a rack of antlers and forms clusters with pointed, brownish yellow tips.

Brain coral

There are several different kinds of brain coral, but in all species the polyps grow together in long rows separated by grooves that resemble the human brain.

Elkhorn coral

Elkhorn coral forms flat, golden branches that look like the wide antlers of an elk. It grows in shallow water, sometimes even sticking out of the water at low tide.

Sharp cups stick out on all the branches, and a diver or snorkeler must be very careful when swimming close to elkhorn coral to avoid getting cut.

Pillar coral

This coral grows in tall columns like a skyscraper or the spires of a cathedral. It looks fuzzy, because the polyps extend their feeding tentacles most of the time.

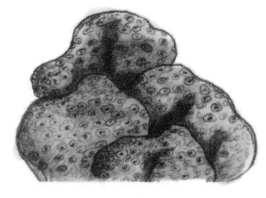

Boulder coral

Boulder coral has a pitted appearance, and it grows in different shapes. Sometimes it looks like a giant bean bag chair, or other times like a head of cabbage.

Soft corals

Soft corals make up a large part of Florida's underwater gardens. Their pleasing colors and gentle shapes, swaying in the current, look like plants growing on or near the reef, but they are coral animals all the same!

They are called soft because they don't create stony cups around their bodies like the hard corals. Instead, spicules—tiny, needlelike pieces of limestone in their tissue—support the polyp's soft body.

Like the hard corals, soft corals grow in different sizes and shapes.

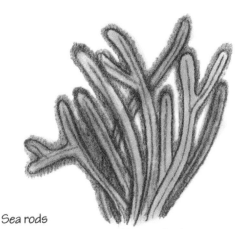

Sea rods
Sea rods are long, sticklike corals that sometimes grow so many branches, they look like underwater bushes.

Sea plumes
Sea plumes, or sea feathers, look like the soft feathers of an ostrich.

Sea fans
Sea fans form delicate, lacy patterns in the shape of a large fan, like the fans that ladies sometimes use to keep cool. They can be purple, yellow, or white.

Sea whips
Sea whips often grow in shallow water far away from the reef. They look like slender whips with their long, thin stalks attached to the hardbottom.

hardbottom rocky areas of the sea floor.
spicules internal skeletal elements of soft corals and sponges.

Coral, Coral, and More Coral!

Some corals can reproduce by releasing millions of microscopic eggs into the water. Some of the eggs ride the ocean currents for hundreds of miles before hatching. After a time, the free-living larvae that hatch from the eggs settle on the ocean floor and change into young coral polyps.

In other species, a small piece of polyp may pinch off to form a new polyp through a process called "budding." These two polyps will produce two more, and those four will produce four more, and so on.

Sometimes coral can be broken during storms or rough seas. If the conditions are just right, these damaged pieces can firmly attach themselves to the sea bottom and grow to become new corals.

reproducing by eggs

budding

Safe circle

Around many patch reefs and large coral heads is a circle of bare white sand called a halo. Grazing fish and sea urchins keep this area clear by feeding on the plant and animal life that lives around the coral. Because this open area can easily be seen by predators, fish venture into it only as far as they feel they can safely go with time for a quick dash back to the reef.

---

budding   developing into a new individual from an outgrowth of the parent.

halo   a ring of white sand surrounding certain corals, caused by grazing marine animals.

Zooxanthellae (say "zoe-uh-zan-THEL-lee")

Each coral polyp shares its home with tiny plants. The plants are a kind of algae called zooxanthellae that live and grow in the tissues of all coral polyps. The name in Greek means "little yellow animal-plant," so they are yellow plants living in an animal.

Zooxanthellae are so dependent on coral that they usually cannot survive in the ocean on their own. They need the coral for food and protection. And likewise, coral polyps use zooxanthellae to make oxygen and food for them. So the algae and the polyp benefit from, and depend upon, each other. This partnership is called symbiosis.

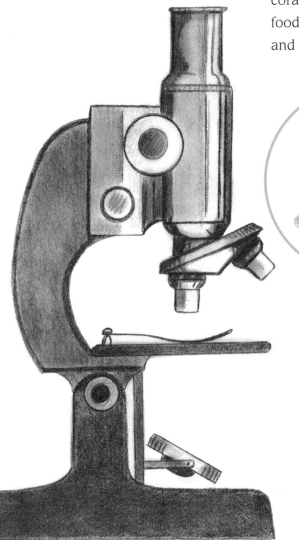

Without zooxanthellae, corals would not have their bright colors. These colors come from the pigments of zooxanthellae rather than from the coral animal itself. In fact, without zooxanthellae, there might not be any coral reefs!

Underwater, the bright colors of a coral reef show all the colors of the rainbow. But seen from the surface of the clear water of the Florida Keys, all reefs look golden brown, and it is hard to tell how deep they are. If you're in a boat and you see brown, you may be about to run aground.

symbiosis *a close relationship between two unlike organisms that live together.*

zooxanthellae *algae that live in the tissues of corals and other organisms.*

Night vs. Day

A reef is like an apartment building, with hollow spaces in between the coral that provide rooms for fish, crabs, and many other animals. But these apartments have two sets of "homeowners."

Some animals feed during the day—either on the reef or in nearby seagrass meadows—and come in at night to rest and sleep in the safety of the reef. Others rest in the reef during the day and take their turn to go out and feed at night.

Day

Night

Sponges

Sponges are everywhere on the reef, living on, under, and even between the corals. A sponge doesn't move about in order to find food, but is a sessile animal that attaches itself to the reef or hardbottom and lets food come to it. Sponges come in a variety of shapes and colors.

Loggerhead sponge

The loggerhead sponge is the largest species of sponge in Florida waters. Its tall, round shape looks like a big barrel or clothes basket. The holes and tunnels inside the sponge provide a safe home for many animals, and sometimes a thousand tiny shrimp live inside a single loggerhead sponge!

Sea anemones

Sea anemones are some of the most beautiful and colorful reef creatures. Like sponges, they can be found growing everywhere on the reef. They are related to the coral polyp, but compared to a tiny polyp, the fist-sized sea anemone is a giant!

Like a sponge, an anemone is a sessile animal, which means that it must grow attached to a hardbottom instead of sand or mud. An anemone will often stick out from a crack or crevice in the reef, its tentacles gently waving to and fro with the currents. But if something frightens it, the anemone will quickly pull its tentacles close to its body.

The tentacles are armed with stinging cells that can kill larger animals that touch them. However, some anemones provide shelter and protection for "guests" that live with the anemone but aren't harmed by its dangerous tentacles.

sessile   referring to animals that require something to attach to.

11

Cleaning shrimp

Cleaning shrimp, so called because they clean parasites off the skin of other animals, often wait at the tip of an anemone's tentacles for a fish to pass by.

One of the cleaning shrimp, the banded coral shrimp, is sometimes called the barber pole shrimp because of its pretty red and white stripes. As it hides among an anemone's tentacles, the shrimp waves its white antennae as a signal to advertise its special cleaning service. A reef fish that is infected with skin-irritating worms or parasites will see this advertising sign and ask for help by using special signals.

The coral shrimp recognizes that the fish is not an enemy, and moves onto the skin of the infected fish to pick away at these irritants. Sometimes several fish will line up at this cleaning station, waiting for their turn to be serviced!

parasite   an organism that lives in or on another
organism, usually causing it harm.

Boring Creatures

Some plants and animals bore holes in the reef, creating ledges, cracks, caves, and tunnels. Creatures that bore holes include certain algae, clams, sponges, and worms.

Even though the actions of these plants and animals damage parts of the reef, the holes they create provide homes for other animals as well as for themselves. Crabs, clams, and worms live in the small holes. Fish and lobsters often hide in the larger, deeper holes near the bottom of the reef.

Christmas tree worm

The Christmas tree worm builds its tube home by boring into live coral. It has a crown of brightly colored tentacles that spreads out in the water to trap plankton. This crown looks just like a miniature Christmas tree. If the worm is disturbed, it snaps back into its tube.

Flamingo tongue snail

Covered with orange and black spots, the flamingo tongue snail feeds on the polyps of sea fans, sticking its tongue into the coral cups and sucking out the living tissue.

Red boring sponge

Most of the boring sponges break down dead coral, but some feed on living coral tissue. The red boring sponge creates holes in the reef by oozing an acid that eats away at dead coral skeletons.

13

Reef Protection

Every animal on the reef has its own special habitat, feeding area, and way of traveling. Some species move between the shallow waters close to the land and the deep waters far offshore. Others live all their lives near a specific type of coral, their bodies designed for feeding only in the narrow cracks and holes of a reef. Many animals also have special ways to protect themselves in their reef homes.

Safety in numbers

Some fish swim alone, seldom leaving the safety of the reef. Others swim together in a large group called a school.

Small fish such as grunts and tangs hover in schools above the reef. An attacking barracuda or grouper finds it very difficult to capture just one fish from such a large crowd. This reduces the chance that any individual fish will be eaten.

Hawksbill sea turtle

The hawksbill sea turtle, named for its hawklike beak, swims in the shallow waters near Florida's coral reefs, where it searches for sponges to eat. The beautiful shell of this turtle has been used to make tortoise-shell jewelry in the past, but now the turtle is protected.

Color

The bright colors of some tropical fish help draw attention to their role in the reef community. In this silent, watery world, color can communicate to others of the same species to stay together in a school. Bright colors can also be a warning to other fish to stay away.

Some species change color as they grow; in others, male and female fish display different colors. Color also helps certain fish blend in with the different backgrounds of the reef.

habitat   the place where a plant or animal naturally grows and lives.

Patterns

Some fish, such as snapper and drum, are hard to see against the reef because spots, stripes, bars, or splotches help to break up the outline of the fish. These unusual patterns may hide important parts of a fish's body.

The four-eye butterflyfish displays two large spots near its tail that look just like eyes. But its real eyes are hidden in a band of black on its head. A predator aims for the false eyes, but misses its chance for a meal when the butterflyfish escapes in the opposite direction.

Now you see me, now you don't

Camouflage color helps protect animals from predators. They blend in with their surroundings, making it difficult for an enemy to see them.

The reef octopus is most often seen crawling along the bottom, searching for crabs to eat while it moves from one hiding place to another. It can change color instantly from red to gray to black to match the background. It can also discharge a jet of black ink to confuse its enemy while it makes a quick escape.

15

Reef Fish

More than 150 species of tropical fish live in and around Florida's coral reefs. Some of Florida's interesting reef fish include:

Angelfish

The angelfish grows as big as a dinner plate and is brightly colored, with a small, pointed mouth to eat crabs, barnacles, and other small invertebrates. Its curious and friendly behavior makes the angelfish one of the diver's favorites. This species is also kept in many saltwater aquariums.

Most angelfish are more colorful when they are young. The juvenile is bright blue and yellow with spots, but loses the spots and becomes an olive-brown color when it grows up.

Sergeant major

The sergeant major is probably the most common reef fish in Florida. Named for its militarylike stripes, it usually swims in schools above the reef, where it feeds on plankton. It darts into the shelter of the reef whenever it feels threatened.

invertebrate   *any animal without a backbone.*

Butterflyfish

Butterflyfish are like teacup saucers in size and shape. They often travel in pairs. Each fish has a long "beak" that it pries into the cracks and crevices of corals and sponges to snap up little crabs and worms.

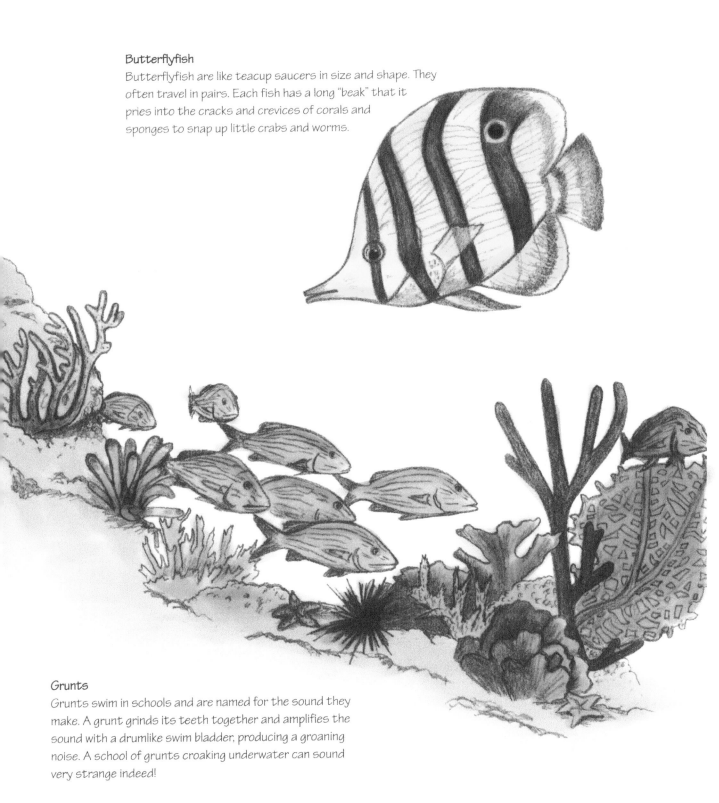

Grunts

Grunts swim in schools and are named for the sound they make. A grunt grinds its teeth together and amplifies the sound with a drumlike swim bladder, producing a groaning noise. A school of grunts croaking underwater can sound very strange indeed!

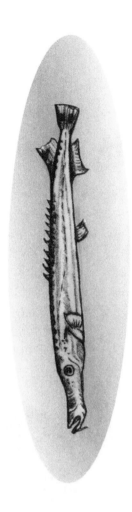

Trumpetfish

The slender trumpetfish hides by floating head down amid the soft sea whips and rods. A small fish swimming by might vanish instantly, inhaled by the lightning-fast gulp of the sneaky trumpetfish.

Squirrelfish

The large eyes and red-orange color of the squirrelfish make it very obvious in bright sunlight. But the squirrelfish lives in the dark tunnels of reef caverns by day, and there its red color appears black, making it hard to see. The squirrelfish comes out into the open water at night, when many other brightly colored reef fish are resting.

Parrotfish

Named for its "beak," which looks like a parrot's, a parrotfish uses its chisel-like teeth to grind large chunks of coral, trying to get at the polyps inside their cup homes. Once the polyps are digested, the skeletons—which by now have been ground into tiny particles—are passed out of the fish's body in a white cloud of sand.

Scientists think that a single parrotfish may crunch enough coral polyps to create more than a ton of sand each year!

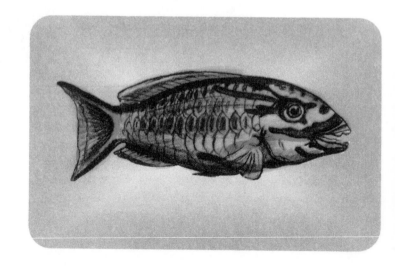

Wrasses

Some fish have colors that attract attention or advertise a special service, much like the cleaning shrimp. A colorful cleaning fish called a wrasse eats harmful parasites on the bodies of much larger fish, who might otherwise be expected to eat the minnow-sized wrasse. Predators recognize the bright colors of cleaners and do not harm them because of the useful service they perform.

Groupers

Huge groupers weighing up to 23 kilograms (50 pounds) lurk around caves and tunnels near the bottom of the reef. With a sudden burst of speed, a grouper can gulp a fish, crab, or lobster into its large mouth. Fishermen like to catch the different kinds of groupers because of their tasty flesh.

19

Reef Neighbors

Coral reefs can't exist by themselves. Like all ecosystems, they are linked to and depend upon other habitats farther away for food and energy. Many animals move between Florida's coral reefs and the mangrove forests and seagrass beds near shore or the deep water habitats far offshore.

Mangrove forests

Not far from the coral reefs, between the land of the Florida Keys and the shallow sea, are the mangrove forests. Three different kinds of mangrove trees grow here, and their roots help to trap the mangrove leaves and other plant detritus that fall or that wash in with the tides.

This leaf litter is broken down into tiny particles by microscopic animals and plants that feed upon the mangrove leaves. The particles are then dissolved in the sea water, where they provide food for filter-feeding sponges and barnacles and detritus feeders such as shrimp. In this way the mangrove forests are the bottom link in the food chain, helping to make food for the animals that live in the shallow waters around the reef.

Mangrove tree roots also provide shelter and hiding places for small fish and crabs. Larger fish move between the mangrove forests and the reef in search of food.

ecosystem   communities of plants and animals that naturally grow and live together.
detritus   particles of decayed animals and plants.

food chain   the passage of food energy from plants, which make their own food from the energy of the sun, to animals that eat plants, to animals that eat other animals.
microscopic   too small to be seen without a magnifying lens.

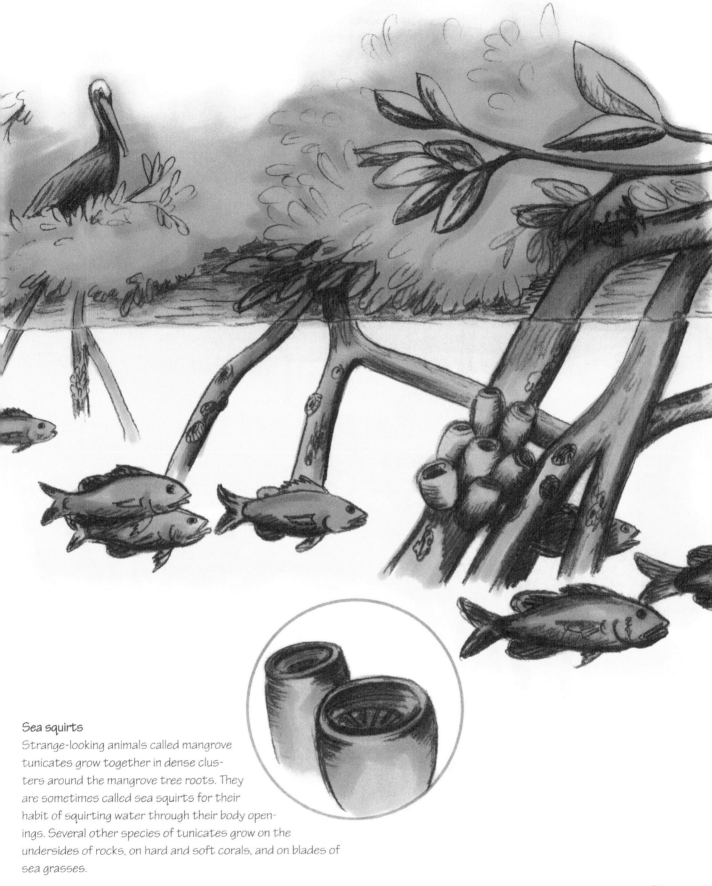

Sea squirts

Strange-looking animals called mangrove tunicates grow together in dense clusters around the mangrove tree roots. They are sometimes called sea squirts for their habit of squirting water through their body openings. Several other species of tunicates grow on the undersides of rocks, on hard and soft corals, and on blades of sea grasses.

Underwater meadows

Sea grasses are flowering plants that live in shallow seas, often close to coral reefs. They form vast underwater meadows that are important to the life cycles of many reef creatures.

Reef fish such as drums and sea bass hatch out and grow up in the seagrass meadows. They move to the reef as adults, but return to the sea grasses to lay their eggs.

Lobsters and snapper hide in the coral reefs during the day and feed in the seagrass meadows at night.

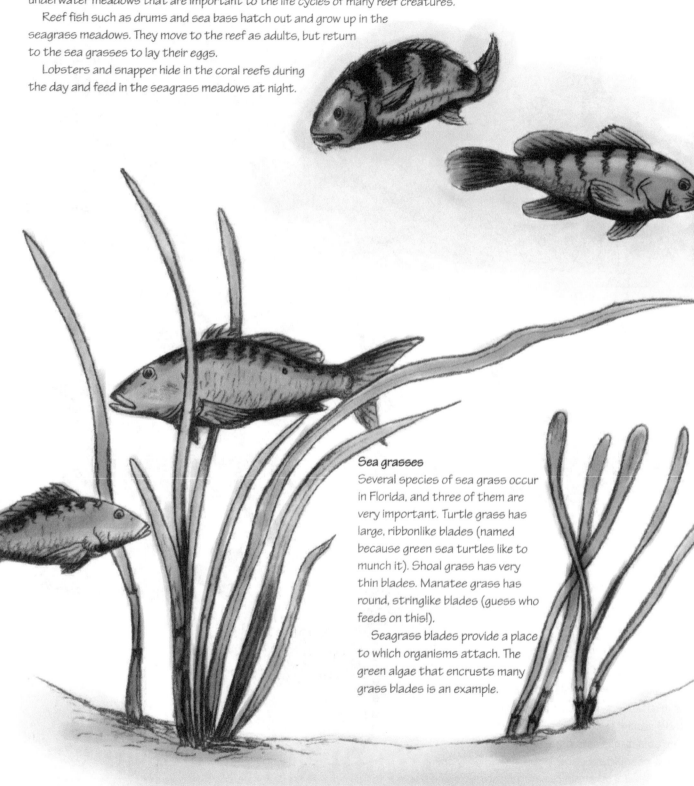

Sea grasses

Several species of sea grass occur in Florida, and three of them are very important. Turtle grass has large, ribbonlike blades (named because green sea turtles like to munch it). Shoal grass has very thin blades. Manatee grass has round, stringlike blades (guess who feeds on this!).

Seagrass blades provide a place to which organisms attach. The green algae that encrusts many grass blades is an example.

Don't call me a starfish!

Sea stars are benthic animals with prickly, spiny, or warty bodies. Some people call them starfish, even though they're not fish at all!

The cushion sea star is easy to see as it glides over the bottom of turtle grass beds. Its large, orange-red body looks like a seat cushion, and it uses its thick, stubby arms to search for snails on the surface of the sand.

Shaving brush algae

The common shaving brush is one of many kinds of algae. It looks like a man's old-fashioned shaving brush growing in the sandy soil near the reef. It has a short stalk topped by a whitish green, brushy head.

Tube worm

The shaggy parchment tube worm covers its paperlike tube home with pieces of shell, mangrove leaves, or pieces of turtle grass blades.

Upside-down jellyfish

The upside-down jellyfish is common in Florida. Sometimes hundreds of them cover the bottom where there is soft, mucky sediment and calm water.

It swims in a normal position for a jellyfish—that is, with its mouth downward—but it soon flops over, settling upside down in shallow water among the sea grasses. In this position, it soaks up the sunshine to turn it into food.

benthic   referring to animals that live on the bottom of the ocean.

Armed and Dangerous

Every animal that lives on the reef could become a meal for someone else. Camouflage coloration helps some reef creatures blend in with their environment, but other animals have developed unusual ways of protecting themselves.

Fire coral

One of the most important corals for swimmers to recognize is fire coral, or stinging coral. If you touch it, it will feel as though you had stuck your finger in a fire, but after a few hours, the pain disappears.

The flat-topped fire coral is common in shallow water and also grows in large areas further offshore. It is easy to recognize with its mustard-yellow color and smooth, flat plates that are squared off at the top.

Moray eel

The spotted moray eel, as thick as a man's arm, slithers in and out of crevices in the reef. It sticks its long body out of a crack and opens a gaping mouth full of fanglike teeth to catch a fish swimming by.

Touch-me-not

Many sponges can cause irritation because of their rough skin. The fire sponge and touch-me-not sponge also contain poison that can cause a burning rash and swollen fingers if a person touches them.

Barracuda

The barracuda has a large mouth filled with razor-sharp teeth for capturing prey. It is streamlined for fast swimming and is one of the larger predators of the reef.

Though ferocious in appearance, it is not always a threat to swimmers or divers. The barracuda is unafraid and curious, and will often approach a diver and even follow one for a while. But even though it will not mistake a diver for a fish, treat the barracuda with respect.

Scorpionfish

The dark, spotted scorpionfish lies motionless on the ocean bottom, blending into the background so well that it is almost invisible. A row of poisonous spines grows beneath the eyes and along the fins to protect the scorpionfish from predators.

Bristles

The bristle worm is related to earthworms and leeches, and crawls about on coral feeding on the polyps. It has soft white patches along its body with needlelike bristles like a porcupine's quills that stick into the flesh of a predator. Also called the fire worm, the bristle worm can cause swimmers very painful wounds that sting for a long time.

Urchins

Sea urchins are slow-moving grazers that feed on blades of turtle grass or scrape algae off the surface of coral.

During the day the long-spined sea urchin hides in the reef under ledges, but at night it comes out to feed in the sea-grass beds. Its needle-sharp spines repel predators and can pierce shoes and swim fins, causing painful puncture wounds.

The Spiny Lobster

Unlike the lobster found in cold waters, the Florida lobster doesn't have large pinching claws. Instead, to protect itself, the animal is covered with spines on its back and antennae and has a horn over each eye. The spiny lobster, sometimes called a crawfish, often sticks its long, brown-and-white, whiplike antennae out from under a ledge of coral. When it moves its antennae rapidly up and down, they produce a rattling noise that warns other lobsters to stay away.

A spiny lobster spends much of its adult life in the coral reef. But in its early life, it drifts in the water currents as a tiny larva in the zooplankton for several months before settling nearer the shore in the seagrass beds.

There the young lobster starts to grow and lives for a while, sometimes inside a loggerhead sponge or under a piece of coral rubble. It may travel between the sea grasses and the mangroves as it feeds, before moving farther offshore to live on a patch reef as a mature adult.

The spiny lobster hides in cracks and holes in the reef during the day, but returns to the seagrass beds at night to feed on small clams, crabs, or dead fish. In the autumn, adult spiny lobsters join together in a large group to travel in a long line—walking head to tail—out to deeper waters offshore.

The numbers of spiny lobsters have declined because too many people like to eat a lobster meal. Now, this species is protected in Florida waters.

zooplankton *animal plankton.*

The Queen of Conchs

The word conch (pronounced "konk") refers to a large group of snails that live throughout the world in shallow, clear seas and seagrass beds near coral reefs. Several species live in Florida, but the queen conch is the largest, nearly as big as a football when fully grown.

Like all other snails, the queen conch secretes a hard shell around itself that protects its soft body. The snail never leaves the shell, but does stretch its foot and head outside in order to move about and feed.

When frightened, the conch withdraws into the safety of its shell, using a horny claw on its foot as a door to keep out intruders.

The conch is a vegetarian that feeds upon algae and detritus by scraping food into its mouth with a hard strip on its tongue called a radula. Although a conch might look as though it's eating sea grass, it is actually feeding on the fine film of algae that grows on the seagrass blades.

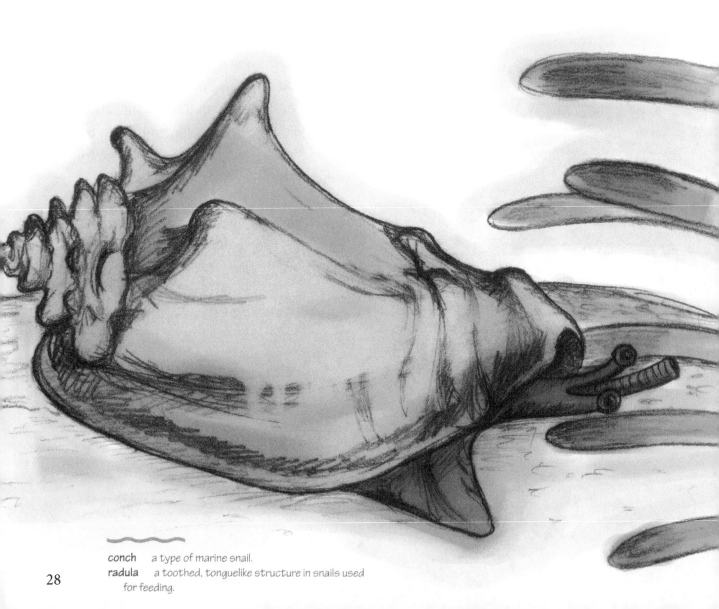

conch   a type of marine snail.
radula   a toothed, tonguelike structure in snails used
    for feeding.

In the summer the queen conch moves great distances to find food in the warm waters. But in the winter, when the shallow seas are rough and cold, the queen conch buries itself in the sand. Sometimes it rests with just the top of its shell sticking out. It may stay that way long enough to become covered with algae and sponges.

Conch is an important seafood, eaten by people as well as many animals, including hawksbill sea turtles, stingrays, spiny lobsters, hermit crabs, and octopuses. Early Native Americans used the conch shell to make tools and pottery. They also made it into a horn by chipping off the tip of the shell and blowing through it.

What Can Harm Florida's Reefs?

Even though it seems as though Florida's coral reefs are as strong as stone walls, able to take anything that nature can toss at them, many things—both natural and human-caused—can harm these fragile habitats.

Natural predators

Parrotfish can damage the coral when they break off chunks of it to feed on the polyps. Long-spined sea urchins graze upon the tiny plants and animals attached to the surface of coral. They also graze on coral larvae, preventing the growth of new polyps. Urchins can completely destroy the reef as they feed, leaving only coral skeletons behind.

Natural forces

Coral can dry out during very low tides, or high waves can wash some soft corals away. Many corals are choked by sand and sediment deposited on top of the reef by storm waves.

During winter cold spells, water temperatures around the reef drop, and the chilly water can harm reef animals, sometimes even killing them.

Disease

Disease can injure and kill corals. One common coral disease is called black band disease. It is caused by bacteria that attack large species, such as boulder coral, when the coral's mucus covering has been damaged such as by parrotfish or a boat anchor. The bacteria then grow by feeding on the coral tissues, forming a dark band as they eat away at the coral.

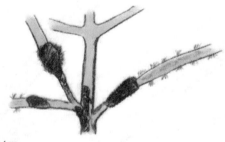

Coral bleaching

Water that is too warm can harm corals, as well as water that is too cold. Coral bleaching occurs when warm water temperatures cause the coral to lose their zooxanthellae. The corals lose their bright colors, and the coral polyps have little energy left for growth.

Why does this happen? Scientists are not sure, but it is known that an increase of only one or two degrees above the usual water temperature can be deadly.

bacteria   microscopic plantlike organisms, many of which cause disease.

sediment   material deposited by water, wind, or waves at the bottom of a body of water.

Conserving Florida's Endangered Reefs

Besides being damaged by nature, coral reefs are too often destroyed by things that humans do. In fact, the world's reefs are being damaged at a faster rate than they can grow back.

Florida's reefs are especially at risk because many people live close to them and many more travel to visit them each year. You can help save the reefs by knowing what causes them harm and doing your part to prevent reef damage.

Be a careful boater

Coral branches can easily be snagged by fishing nets, traps, and anchor lines, or broken by a boat's anchor, hull, or propeller.

Mooring buoys are floats carefully installed near some Florida reefs. Boaters can tie their boats to the buoys and never need to drop anchor on the reef. If you go for a boating trip with your family, always use a mooring buoy if one is available instead of the anchor.

Also when boating, never throw overboard tangled fishing line or other litter that can become trapped on the reef. Take it home with you to dispose of properly.

Swim responsibly

Snorkelers and scuba divers cause coral damage when they stand on or hold onto the coral. When you are swimming or snorkeling, remember that coral is a colony of tiny living animals and be careful not to touch it.

Take only pictures!

The beautiful colors of living coral reef animals soon fade when they are removed from their ocean home, so leave all creatures where you find them. Catch your animal with an underwater camera instead!

If we all do our best to protect the ocean environment, the beauty of these underwater gardens can be enjoyed by all who visit Florida's coral reefs.

Glossary

algae (AL-jee)   certain plants that usually live in water.

bacteria   microscopic plantlike organisms, many of which cause disease.

benthic   referring to animals that live on the bottom of the ocean.

budding   developing into a new individual from an outgrowth of the parent.

colony   a group of the same kind of animal living together.

conch (konk)   a type of marine snail.

detritus (de-TRY-tus)   particles of decayed animals and plants.

ecosystem (EE-ko-sis-tum)   communities of plants and animals that naturally grow and live together.

food chain   the passage of food energy from plants, which make their own food from the energy of the sun, to animals that eat plants, to animals that eat other animals.

graze   to feed on vegetation.

habitat   the place where a plant or animal naturally grows and lives.

halo   a ring of white sand surrounding certain corals caused by grazing marine animals.

hardbottom   rocky areas of the sea floor.

invertebrate   any animal without a backbone.

larva (plural: larvae [LARV-eye])   the immature form of an animal that is very different from its adult form.

microscopic   too small to be seen without a magnifying lens.

mucus   a slimy protective secretion.

nematocysts (nee-MAT-uh-sists)   stinging cells in tentacles of coral polyps, jellyfish, and anemones.

organic   made of living (or formerly living) plants or animals.

parasite   an organism that lives in or on another organism, usually causing it harm.

plankton   microscopic plants and animals that drift in the sea.

polyp (PAUL-lip)   a marine animal with a tubelike body which is attached at one end to a hard surface and which has a mouth at the other end.

predator   an animal that hunts, kills, and eats other animals.

prey   an animal that is eaten by another animal.

radula   a toothed, tonguelike structure in snails used for feeding.

rubble   pieces of broken coral.

secrete   to release a substance.

sediment   material deposited by water, wind, or waves at the bottom of a body of water.

sessile (SESS-ul)   referring to animals that require something to attach to.

species (SPEE-sheez)   a kind of plant or animal.

spicules   internal skeletal elements of soft corals and sponges.

subtropical   situated in the region of the earth lying between the tropics and temperate lands (cooler than the tropics, warmer than the temperate areas)

symbiosis   a close relationship between two unlike organisms that live together.

tentacles   a ring of food-gathering appendages surrounding the mouth of some marine animals.

tropical   situated in the tropics, a part of the earth's surface near the equator where it is very warm.

zooplankton (ZOE-uh-plank-ton)   animal plankton.

zooxanthellae (zoe-uh-zan-THEL-lee)   algae that live in the tissues of corals and other organisms.

CPSIA information can be obtained at www.ICGtesting.com
Printed in the USA
BVOW10s0540160414

PP5725600001B/1/P

9 781561 647033